HELPING

by Jane Buerger and Jennie Davis
illustrated by Kathryn Hutton

Mankato, MN 56001

Library of Congress Cataloging in Publication Data

Buerger, Jane, 1922-
   Helping.

   (What is it?)
   Rev. ed. of: Helping is— . © 1984.
   Summary: Suggests ways of caring for other people
and being helpful to family members, friends, and
others.
   1. Caring—Moral and ethical aspects—Juvenile
literature.   2. Helping behavior—Moral and ethical
aspects—Juvenile literature.   [1. Helpfulness.
2. Christian life]   I. Hutton, Kathryn, ill.
II. Buerger, Jane, 1922-   .   Helping is— .
BJ1475.B84   1985   241'.4   84-23750
ISBN 0-89565-302-8 -1991 Edition

Helping means caring for others . . .
like when my little sister is sick
and I stay inside to play with her
—even though my friends are jumping
rope just outside my window.

When my little sister is pulling
her wagon up the hill, and I push
from behind, that's helping!

And helping is holding up a friend
when he is learning to skate.

Helping is eating my vegetables and
drinking my milk . . .

ANGRY

and holding Baby Brother on my lap
when Mom reads a story.

When Baby Brother is sleeping, helping is tiptoeing by his door.

Helping is wiping up spilled milk.

Helping is picking up my clothes
and putting them in the hamper.

Helping is washing my hands after
making mud pies.

When the bird bath is dry, helping is
filling it with water.

Helping is taking care of my kitty.
It's feeding her and giving her fresh
water. It's also brushing her fur.

When Dad washes the car, helping is rubbing it 'til it shines.

When company is coming for dinner,
helping is folding the napkins—very
carefully.

When our neighbors are away on
vacation and it hasn't rained, helping
is watering their roses.

Helping is doing hard things cheer-
fully—such as going to the doctor
or dentist.

Being helpful means caring about others. It's helping to fill a Thanksgiving basket . . .

or taking dinner to a neighbor who is
sick.

Helping is shoveling snow off the
front walk, so no one will slip . . .

and then wiping the snow off my
boots before going inside.

Helping is passing out the bells
at music time.

Helping is sharing my books and toys.

Helping is caring for one another
every day.
Can you think of other ways to be
helpful?